Original title:
The Paradise of the Ocean

Copyright © 2025 Creative Arts Management OÜ
All rights reserved.

Author: Adrian Caldwell
ISBN HARDBACK: 978-1-80581-585-3
ISBN PAPERBACK: 978-1-80581-112-1
ISBN EBOOK: 978-1-80581-585-3

Echoes of Aquatic Serenity

Fish in tuxedos dance with glee,
While crabs in shades sip iced sea tea.
Dolphins laugh, flipping in the air,
And seaweed sways like it's at a fair.

Jellyfish jelly on the buffet,
Squid serenades make us sway.
Octopus cooks with eight fine hands,
While seashells form quite the marching bands.

Beneath the Glittering Surface

Starfish belting out tunes so sweet,
While clam chowder takes a seat.
Mermaids sing a silly song,
As bubbles drift and fish catch on.

Anemones sway in stylish flair,
While snails have races with no care.
Crustaceans argue, who's the best,
And seahorses never take a rest.

Secrets of the Coral Kingdom

Chubby pufferfish puff up wide,
Nemo's antics, they cannot hide.
Corals gossip, knitting reefs,
While turtles nap, oblivious thieves.

Clownfish joke with a tiny grin,
The ocean's laughter, where to begin?
Starfish throw confetti in delight,
As schools of fish swim left and right.

A Haven of Salt and Light

Sandy snacks in a conch shell plate,
Barnacles have a restaurant fate.
Urchins play cards with a wink and a nod,
While stingrays zoom past, it's quite a façade.

Seashells chuckle with tales to share,
Sea cucumbers lounge without a care.
Lobsters dancing in top hats bright,
This underwater jam is pure delight.

Celestial Watercolors

Dancing waves in shades of blue,
Crabs wear hats and sing a tune.
Seashells giggle on the sand,
Fish making art with their own hands.

Starfish brush with polka dots,
Turtles racing with funny thoughts.
Octopus juggling pearls with flair,
While dolphins trade their wildest hair.

A Voyage Through Aquamarine

On a boat made of jellybeans,
Sailing past the seaweed scenes.
Gummy sharks and fizzy drinks,
Mermaids whisper, 'What do you think?'

With each wave, a ticklish breeze,
Clams tell jokes that bring you ease.
Sardines dance in synchronized,
Their shimmering scales—what a surprise!

Secrets Beneath the Surface

Beneath the waves, a secret show,
Squids wearing glasses and clownfish glow.
Grumpy turtles with frowning faces,
Playing checkers in muddy spaces.

Anemones waltz to a funky beat,
Shrimp do salsa on their tiny feet.
Waves are giggling, the sun's a clown,
Life's a circus when you're underwater town!

The Call of the Sirens

Sirens sing with ice-cream cones,
Balancing treats while casting tones.
They lure sailors with candy calls,
While seagulls steal their french fries and balls.

Bubble-blowing fish in a line,
Tickle each other, feel divine.
Sea cucumbers wear silly hats,
Laughing at haters, saying, 'That's that!'

Armor of the Ocean

In the depths, a crab wears a hat,
Says, "I'm the king! How about that?"
A starfish taps its speckled feet,
Doing a jig, oh what a treat!

Flip-flops float, they dance with glee,
As dolphins sing, 'Join the spree!'
A sea turtle dons a quirky tie,
And all the fish just wave goodbye!

A Dance with Sea Serpents

Sea serpents twirl in sparkling trance,
With bubbles, they lead a bubbly dance.
Octopus plays the accordion loud,
While the seahorses form a proud crowd.

They twine and swirl, what a sight to see,
Singing out, 'Come dance with me!'
With a splash, they slip and slide,
In this ocean ball, all worries subside!

Glimmering Grotto

In a grotto where jellyfish glow,
The party's hopping, go with the flow!
Clams snap their jaws, making a beat,
While seaweed dancers sway to the heat.

A clam in a top hat shouts, 'Surprise!'
As shrimp jump up in silly ties.
The two-lipped fish giggle and tease,
Letting loose like a gentle breeze!

Intrigue Under Water

With whispers and giggles, the fish convene,
Plotting a prank on a flat-headed queen.
A pufferfish puffed up with glee,
Said, "Watch out for mischief; oh, just wait and see!"

They plotted and planned with sneaky delight,
As a seagull swooped down, what a fright!
With a squawk and a giggle, they all took flight,
In the ocean's deep realm, make mischief tonight!

Whispers Beneath the Waves

In the deep where fishy jokes flow,
Sea cucumbers giggle, don't you know?
Starfish argue who has the best flair,
While dolphins practice their stand-up air.

Octopus plays games, with jokes in his ink,
His arms confuse even the smartest of thinkers.
With each joke he weaves, the bubbles all cheer,
As sea turtles roll, laughing without a fear.

Depths of Dreams Unfurled

The jellyfish dance with their wobbly grace,
While clams put on spectacles, thinking they're ace.
Anemones giggle, tickling their pals,
As clownfish swim by, telling hilarious tales.

Sardines swerve, and their antics ensue,
Crabs in tuxedos say, "What's new with you?"
With bubbles above them and laughter below,
These fish have a party where humor keeps flow.

Tides of Tranquility Embrace

The seashell choir sings off-key in delight,
Mermaids giggle, planning pranks every night.
With waves that tickle, and tides that tease,
The fish all unite for some jokes 'neath the breeze.

Seahorses trot with their comical style,
While barnacles gossip with laughter and guile.
Sandcastles chuckle as the waves start to play,
In this silly abode where smiles never fray.

Celestial Currents of Blue

Stars twinkle down like fishy confetti,
While ocean snails slide, their motions quite sweaty.
Wave after wave, they tumble and roll,
With shrimp making jokes, they're on a fishy stroll.

The sun's laughter ripples, painting all gold,
While sea otters plot, they're never too bold.
Each current tells tales of joy, fun, and cheer,
In this watery world, where laughter draws near.

Revelations in the Riptide

In a seaweed suit, I took a dive,
Fins and flip-flops, quite the jive.
A starfish winked, said, "What's the deal?"
I laughed so hard, I lost my meal.

Jellyfish danced with electric flair,
Tangled my legs in a sticky snare.
A crab said, "Buddy, this is your plight!"
As I tried to float, the fish took flight.

Fluttering Mirages of Marine Life

I spied a dolphin in a top hat,
Waving to fish in a goldfish chat.
They laughed at me, bobbing in glee,
"Join the parade! Come swim, oh whee!"

The sea cucumbers, all in a row,
Said, "Pick up the pace, let's put on a show!"
A clownfish chuckled, "What's your best trick?"
I floundered about, looking quite sick.

Dances of the Deep Blue

In the depths where the sun seldom peeks,
Fish threw confetti, played hide and seek.
An octopus twirled, what a bright sight!
He juggled his limbs, much to my delight.

With shells for a stage, they flaunted their flair,
Turtles slow-danced, with stylish care.
The seashells clapped as waves rolled along,
While I, the audience, sang a fishy song.

Serene Sanctuaries and Whispering Waves

Coral castles with doors that squeak,
Mother clam snoring, oh so unique!
Seahorses riding on bubbles of fun,
While pufferfish danced under the sun.

Anemones giggled, tickling the tide,
Making the fish blushingly hide.
Here in the splash of the ocean's sweet kiss,
Every wave says, "You won't want to miss!"

Diver's Lament

Oh, I dove deep and lost my gear,
A fish swam by and pointed, 'Here!'
I tried to chase it, but oh dear,
I ended up with seaweed near.

My goggles fogged up, I couldn't see,
Bumping into a stinging bee.
I thought it was a jelly, whee!
Turns out it's just my friend Chuckie.

I waved goodbye to passing crabs,
They stole my sandwich and some tabs.
Next time I'll pack my snacks in slabs,
To deal with all these ocean jabs.

So if you dive, my friends, take heed,
Leave snacks at home, that's my good creed.
Laughter echoes with a seaweed bead,
Life's just currents, swimming free indeed!

Fragments of an Underwater Ballet

Dancing jellyfish, what a sight,
Twirling like they own the night.
Shoals of fish in sheer delight,
    Just trying to avoid a bite.

A crab in tights, oh what a scene,
Waltzing through the kelp so green.
He slips and trips, an awkward glean,
    His partner's face is quite serene.

Starfish pirouette with grace,
Missing limbs, but keep the pace.
They're not blue, just lost in space,
    In undersea, a comical race.

The sea turtle joins with flair,
Doing corkscrews without a care.
I laugh so hard, I splash a mare,
In this ballet, fun's everywhere!

Mysteries of the Marianas

Down in the depths where darkness lurks,
Squid play poker, no need for jerks.
They bluff and blink with sly smirks,
Gambling for shiny, ancient perks.

A mermaid sings to lost sailors,
But they're just fish in improvised trailers.
With underwater tales like jailers,
Gossiping about sunken wailers.

The great trench hides a treasure trove,
But finding it's a tricky grove.
I fished for pearls in the bright cove,
Instead I caught a seal who grove.

The ocean whispers, secrets tight,
Creatures giggle in the fading light.
In this abyss, all's silly, bright,
Life's a splash in a wild fight!

Skipping Stones at Dusk

At dawn, I tossed a pebble far,
It landed with a perfect 'blar'.
Watched it skip, like a bouncing car,
Joining crabs in a dance bizarre.

Clouds above like cotton candy,
While fish below are feeling dandy.
I threw a stone, but oh so handy,
A turtle caught it, what a shandy!

The waves giggled, splashing me,
As I tried to launch with glee.
Instead, I tripped and fell, you see,
Now I'm part of the ocean spree!

So next time, skip your stones with fun,
But watch out for those waves that run.
Join the dance, don't be outdone,
Laughter flows when the day is done!

Radiance of the Turquoise Sea

The waves wore sunglasses, oh so cool,
Splashing around, like a playful fool.
Fish in tuxedos danced on the floor,
Screaming, "Who needs land? We want more!"

Seashells held meetings in their own way,
Deliberating on how much to play.
Starfish gossiping about seaweed fries,
Crabs drawing maps to their favorite pies.

Embraced by an Ocean's Embrace

Seagulls cracking jokes, they take a dive,
Splashing the surfers who try to thrive.
The sunbeams laugh as they bounce on the sea,
While dolphins wiggle, as happy as can be!

Turtles in flip-flops stroll down the shore,
Holding beach parties, they always want more.
With shells as their speakers, they crank up the tunes,
While crabs cha-cha beneath the bright moons.

Whispers of the Tides

The tides had a secret, whispered in glee,
"Mermaids are real, come surf with me!"
They painted the waves with colors so bright,
And invited the fish for a late-night flight.

Octopuses knitting under the waves,
Making long scarves for all of the braves.
Jellyfish hopscotched through bubbles and sprays,
While sea urchins laughed at their clumsy ways.

Secrets Beneath the Waves

A treasure chest giggles, it knows so much,
Filled with lost socks and a rubber duck.
The reef is a dance floor of neon delight,
Where sea cucumbers get groovy at night.

Clownfish telling jokes to the pufferfish crew,
Their laughter a melody, treble and true.
The crabs play leapfrog, what a wild sight,
In this underwater realm, everything's bright!

Kaleidoscopic Waters

Bubbles pop and dance in glee,
Fish wear hats made stylishly.
Crabs do salsa on the sand,
While seagulls clap, a merry band.

Shells are secrets, gossiping,
Starfish juggle with a zing.
Turtles race in silly games,
Waving flags with silly names.

Mirrored waves with laughter ring,
Jellyfish in a conga fling.
An octopus spins tales so tall,
As sea cucumbers take a fall.

In this realm of wacky tides,
Nautical jokes the ocean hides.
With spray and foam, joy is found,
In the splash of fun all around.

The Eternal Pulse of the Sea

Waves come crashing with a cheer,
Shrimp in tuxedos waltz near.
A dolphin dons a bowler hat,
While seaweed forms a welcome mat.

A clam is posing like a star,
While crabs ride scooters, oh how bizarre!
Barnacles share a pirate's tale,
In a world where fish go to jail.

Pelicans fish with flair and grace,
While sea stars play a game of chase.
Blowfish puff, their cheeks so round,
In this wacky, wet playground.

So come and join, don't be shy,
Wave your fins and say goodbye!
As the surf jokes, we all agree,
Nothing's funnier than the sea!

Reflections of the Shimmering Sea

Mermaids laugh as they frolic free,
Winking at fish with a cup of tea.
Seagulls squawk in funny tones,
While starfish dance on coral thrones.

A whale sings notes that creak and bend,
As sardines twist and break the trend.
Waves like giggles lap the shore,
Who knew the sea could chuckle more?

Bubble parties host the best,
With crabs cracking jokes, no time to rest.
Fish form choirs, scale by scale,
In the shimmering depths, we all prevail.

Anchor your worries, come have a blast,
In this place where time flies fast.
For laughter echoes, bright and clear,
In this zany world we hold dear.

Land of Endless Blue

Puddles splash, who'd thought it true,
That silly fishes wear sunglasses too?
With a wink and a flip of the tail,
They spin stories that never stale.

An octopus waves from a pearly shell,
Sporting a smile, it's doing well.
Whimsical waves make giggles swell,
As even the seaweed wishes to yell!

Crabs play tag on the sandy beach,
Each with a lesson that they'd teach.
With a flick of the fin, they rush and roam,
In the blue expanse, they call it home.

Join this circus, don't just stand by,
Where the ocean laughs and kids can fly.
All aboard for a jolly spree,
In this wonderful world, so wild and free!

Serenade of the Sea Glass

Bottles float with tales to tell,
Seaweed dances, under a shell.
Crabs wear hats, silly and tight,
Laughing as they scuttle out of sight.

Starfish line up for a show,
With bright pink wigs, putting on a glow.
Seagulls cackle, a feathery choir,
As waves clap hands, never tire.

Jellyfish jiggle like they're in a spin,
Playing tag, with the tide they win.
Sandcastles wobble, see them collapse,
A royal court of sandy chaps!

At sunset, clams toss confetti bright,
Seashells enjoy the party with delight.
Underneath the sky, giggles arise,
In the quirky kingdom of water-wise.

Blue Horizons Unfolding

The horizon stretches, a canvas of cheer,
Where dolphins leap, spreading good vibes here.
Seashells whisper secrets, quite absurd,
While fish in tuxedos waltz, undeterred.

Waves crash like laughter, no need for a frown,
Surfboards and sea stars parade through town.
A clam in sunglasses sips saltwater tea,
While turtles joke about setting up a spree.

Gulls swoop down, wearing tiny boots,
Dancing on drifts of old fishy fruits.
With a wink and a flip, they steal the scene,
In this ocean of fun, like a dream machine.

Every splash brings a giggle and cheer,
As crabs play the drums, inviting you near.
Under the sun, let laughter abound,
In the joyful splash of the ocean's sound.

Moonlit Waves

Under the moon, the waves play tricks,
A dance of shadows, a comedy mix.
Fish in tuxedos throw a grand ball,
While shrimps do the limbo, amusing us all.

The lighthouse winks like a mischievous friend,
As starfish spread rumors, they never end.
Octopus pranks with a cheeky grin,
Playing chess while fish try to fit in.

Crabs tell tall tales, pincer to pincer,
About the massive fish they couldn't out-wince her.
At the tide's edge, laughter echoes and sways,
In the moonlit frolic of funny sea plays.

With each tiny wave, the jokes cascade,
In this shimmering world, where fun's never mislaid.
When night descends, under silvery beams,
The ocean spins laughter, stitching our dreams.

Treasure of the Tidepools

Puddles of joy, where creatures convene,
A treasure chest brimming with laughter unseen.
With crabs in sunglasses and snails on the way,
They plan a parade for the next sunny day.

The sea cucumbers wiggle with glee,
As children discover the wonder and spree.
Anemones wave like they're beckoning in,
"Come join the fun, let the swim begin!"

Starfish do cartwheels, oh what a sight,
While mussels hold hands, enjoying the night.
Sea urchins gossip about the day's haul,
As friends bounce around, creating a ball.

With every tide, new jesters arise,
Swapping their wigs under bright sunny skies.
In this pool of giggles, each finds their role,
For here in the tide, there's joy for the soul.

Land of the Endless Tide

Waves are dancing, what a sight,
A fish in sunglasses, oh so bright!
Crabs in shells, they strut with pride,
Doing the cha-cha, side by side.

Seagulls gossip, they squawk and tease,
While turtles glide with graceful ease.
Starfish play games of hide and seek,
With jellyfish that tickle your cheek.

Beach balls tumble, laughter's loud,
As dolphins leap and mischief's proud.
Witty shells whisper soft sea jokes,
While seaweed sways and gently pokes.

Oh, what fun this watery land,
Where everyone's got a silly plan!
Under the sun, just take a dive,
In this ocean where we thrive!

Radiance of the Ocean's Embrace

The sun sings softly, waves come alive,
A clam with a hat, ready to jive.
Octopus painting with colors so bold,
While fish tell tales that never grow old.

Crabs on parade, a marching band,
With shells so shiny, looking so grand.
Seashells giggle, they share a joke,
As coral reefs begin to poke.

Whales send texts in bubble streams,
While sea turtles swim in their dreams.
A dance-off starts with a splash and dive,
In seaweed wigs, they come alive!

Who knew the ocean could be this fun?
With laughter echoing, everyone runs.
Flip-flops flinging, sunscreen's out,
In this watery land, we laugh and shout!

Fluttering Fin Tales

With fins so flashy and tails that twirl,
Fish in tuxedos ready to swirl.
A pufferfish dresses in polka dots,
As sea cucumbers tell funny plots.

Shrimps in line for the dance-off scene,
Twisting and turning, they look so keen!
Whimsical waves with a shimmer and shake,
As barnacles giggle, they just can't break.

Moonlit nights bring a carnival glow,
Where squids juggle while anemones flow.
Clownfish acting, they steal the show,
With sea urchin friends, they steal the flow!

In this realm where laughter swims free,
Every wave whispers joy, can't you see?
Let's join this party, come take a chance,
In funny fin tales, we all shall dance!

Silent Song of the Deep

Fish dance in circles, quite absurd,
With fins that flap and tails unheard.
A crab plays drums on a conch shell,
While seaweed sways, under a spell.

The octopus juggles, oh what a sight,
With eight arms flailing, in pure delight.
A dolphin giggles, leaping high,
Waving to turtles that float by.

Anemones blush in colorful hues,
Tickling the toes of snoozing blues.
A clownfish tells jokes, puns abound,
As sea stars laugh without a sound.

Bubbles rise up like little balloons,
As squids play hide and seek with the moons.
In the kingdom below, humor is king,
Where every fish joins in to sing.

The Ocean's Gentle Breath

Waves whisper secrets to the shore,
As starfish stretch and crabs encore.
A whale tells tales of voyages grand,
While shrimp breakdance on shifting sand.

Seagulls squawk with snappy remarks,
Debating where to find the best parks.
The jellyfish float, a ghostly crew,
Trying to tickle a passing shoe.

Clowning around in a kelp-made maze,
The sea cucumbers join in the craze.
With surfing sea otters, catching some rays,
Every tide brings unending plays.

Under the waves, where laughter's a caper,
Life's a wild show, without any taper.
In salty waters, joy's always found,
Where every splash brings giggles around.

Nautical Whispers

Mermaids gossip, with flicks of their tails,
In bubbles of laughter, their joy never fails.
A fish on a skateboard rolls with some flair,
While turtles take selfies, showing they care.

An anglerfish grins, a quirky old chap,
Wearing a light as a flashy cap.
The pufferfish booms, puffed up with pride,
While eels give each other a lively slide.

Coral reefs chuckle, a colorful crew,
As each brings a joke that's utterly new.
With playful plankton and hiding sea snails,
The humor is deep, in these salty trails.

Beneath the waves, there's never a frown,
With laughter that echoes, all around town.
The ocean smiles wide, with giggles that swell,
In waters so merry, it casts a spell.

Beneath the Starry Waters

In the night, the sea shines bright,
With winking fish, oh what a sight!
The moonbeams dance on waves so high,
While sea horses trot, none shy to try.

A grouper steals a sunken shoe,
Claiming his throne, it's now his zoo.
Anemones giggle, a ticklish bunch,
Waiting for crabs to join the lunch.

A blowfish jokes, what a ham,
As eels all laugh, 'That's not a clam!'
With laughter floating through the deep,
They wink at the stars, in joy they leap.

So come take a dip, where mirth runs free,
In waters that bubble with glee and spree.
For every splash brings a story to cheer,
In this underwater world, where fun is near.

Oceanic Daydreams

Sandy toes and flip-flops on,
Seagulls squawk like crazy bawn.
Waves laugh with a bubbly cheer,
While crabs dance like they have no fear.

Beach balls bouncing in the sun,
Kids are screaming, oh what fun!
Fish swim by in a silly race,
Winking at each other's face.

Sunscreen battles, who's got more?
Slather it on from head to floor.
Mermaids giggle, tails a-shine,
Wishing for a beach cabana wine.

Toward the horizon with a grin,
Chasing jellyfish that swim in spin.
Ocean's quirks, a cosmic jest,
Ready, set, let's dive, who's the best?

Luminous Seafoam

Glowing foam on waves that stray,
Whispers secrets of the day.
Mermaids laughing, oh so bright,
Dancing 'neath the moon's soft light.

Starfish playing tag and chase,
In this wacky, funny space.
Octopus with eight arms flail,
Conducting songs, a hippy whale.

The clams hold court, they play it cool,
While sea turtles slide, breaking rule.
Crabs composing symphonies,
Shells clink like wild tambourines.

With flippered friends, we take a dive,
In this world, we feel alive.
Each splash a giggle, every wave a jest,
In luminous antics, we feel blessed.

Depths of Tranquility

Underwater, where bubbles pop,
Fishy faces never stop.
A turtle with a wise old wink,
Offers pearls, but what do you think?

Colder depths bring a chill of surprise,
As squids trip over their own supplies.
Eels are tangled in a doggone knot,
While sunken ships ask, 'What have I got?'

Coral reefs twist in a fun ballet,
Playing hide and seek all day.
Crabs in tuxedos, oh what a sight,
Celebrate with a dance each night.

Even the starfish join the dance,
As dolphins prance in ocean's trance.
In this stillness, laughter floats,
Nature's joke, like playful boats.

Crystalline Waters

Crystal clear, the ocean's laugh,
A dolphin's doing the math.
Calculating jumps and flips,
While sardines form little ships.

Clams are gossiping, "Did you see?"
How sea lettuce flirts with the sea?
The sea anemones swish and sway,
Waving hello to the light of day.

With flippers, we frolic without a care,
Fish telling tales of their scandalous affair.
Whales hum tunes that make us grin,
In this watery world, let laughter begin.

As rays of sun dance on the bay,
We splash around, forgetting the fray.
Each drop sparkles like a frothy cheer,
In crystalline vibes, we have no fear!

Echoes of Marine Melody

Bubbles dancing in the breeze,
Fish in tuxedos trying to tease,
Seagulls giggle, doing their routine,
Splashing water like a fountain machine.

Crabs hosting a waltz on the sand,
Starfish juggling, oh so grand,
Octopuses knitting with seaweed flair,
As dolphins join in without a care.

Turtles in shades, cruising with style,
Whales tell jokes that make you smile,
A clownfish cracks a pun so sly,
While jellyfish float on by, oh my!

Underwater, there's a comedy show,
With a sea cucumber as the star of the flow,
Coral reefs throw a party each night,
Where laughter echoes and hearts feel light.

The Hidden Coral Kingdom

In oceans deep, a realm so bright,
Coral castles stand in delight,
Fish parade in colors all around,
Where silly sea creatures abound.

Shrimp perform a tap dance fair,
With anemones caught in their hair,
Clownfish trading quips left and right,
While crabs try to dance, what a sight!

The sea cucumbers think they're cool,
But the blowfish just plays the fool,
Eels have jokes that twist and turn,
Making the oysters giggle and churn.

In this kingdom, laughter rules the tide,
With ticklish sponges to tickle your side,
Join the fun, don't miss the show,
With a wave of the fin, get ready to go!

Waves of Wonder

Splashing surf with a humorous quirk,
Fish doing tricks like it's no big work,
Seaweed sways like it knows the beat,
While crabs tap dance with mighty feet.

Seashells gossip, oh what a tale,
Of pirates who tried but always did fail,
Starfish spin yarns of their wild escapades,
While sea otters bask in sunlit parades.

A friendly dolphin blows bubbles so grand,
While snails complain about getting to land,
The tides are chuckling, the waves are alive,
In this watery world where jokes will thrive.

Laughter breaks on the shore like foam,
Creating a home where all creatures roam,
In every splash, in every swirl,
A comic ocean, what a world!

Companions of the Current

In currents swift, the pals unite,
A dolphin spins, what a sight!
A sardine tells a secret so silly,
As sea urchins collect pearls for a filly.

With turtles that race and crabs that boast,
A plankton party, oh what a coast,
Clownfish chatter, while anemones sway,
A merry band at play every day.

Coral reefs filled with glee and delight,
As fish make jokes that feel just right,
The ocean's pulse a rhythm of cheer,
Where every ripple brings laughter near.

Join the fun, take a swim, dive deep,
In this world, no need for sleep,
For companions of water, oh what a thrill,
A funny ocean, where joy never still.

Embracing the Ocean's Heart

I met a fish with a funny grin,
It wore a hat, said it's a fin!
It danced and twirled, a true delight,
I laughed so hard, it took to flight.

The seaweed waved like it knew the joke,
A crab did a jig, then nearly broke!
With dolphins laughing, all in a heap,
The ocean's laughter, oh so deep!

Serenade of the Silver Sands

On silver shores with sandals bright,
I tripped on shells, oh what a sight!
The sandcastles crumbled, with a boom,
A pharaoh crab claimed the room!

Seagulls squawked in a comical tune,
While sunbathers melted, like cheese in June.
A turtle in shades rolled by with flair,
"Don't rush," it said, "there's sea everywhere!"

Journey to the Glistening Abyss

I dove with goggles, couldn't see clear,
A fish yelled, "Watch out!" with a smirk and a cheer!
A lost pair of fins helped me float,
While a squid squiggled off with my tote!

Underwater selfies with a starfish friend,
Kept posing and laughing, it wouldn't end.
Bubbles bubbled up like popcorn, oh joy!
"Let's strike a pose!" said the starfish, coy!

Aquatic Dreams in Sapphire Tides

In sapphire waves, where mermaids play,
I found a whale who loved ballet!
It spun and flipped with quite the grace,
While clams applauded from their safe space.

An octopus offered me a drink,
In a coconut cup, made me think!
"Hold your breath," it giggled, "Don't be shy!
The sea's our stage, come give it a try!"

Depths of Forgotten Dreams

In the depths where sunken ships lie,
Old socks swim and seagulls fly.
Mermaids giggle, sipping sea foam,
While crabs waltz and make it their home.

Octopuses juggle with shiny pearls,
As fish play poker, flipping their swirls.
The laughter echoes, bubbles rise high,
In this watery world, dreams never die.

Turtles in shades, doing the cha-cha,
While dolphins dance like they've hit the radar.
Seaweed sways to the rhythm of fun,
In this joyful place, we all come undone.

So dive down deep, join the crazy show,
Where the fish hold court and crabs steal the glow.
Forget your worries, let the tides sweep,
As we swim in laughter, oceans run deep.

Chirping Crickets by the Shore

Crickets chirp to the rhythm of waves,
While sandcastles grow like the mind misbehaves.
Seagulls squawk in a karaoke blast,
As beach balls roll and summer screams fast.

Lizards tan on rocks, donning shades,
Planning their parties with sun-kissed parades.
While the tide's a DJ with conch shell spins,
And everyone dances, where the fun begins.

The flip-flops are flying, the laughter's contagious,
As seashells serenade with voices outrageous.
With crickets as guides, we all join the fray,
In this sandy retreat, we laugh night and day.

So toast to the waves and the chirps in the night,
As fireflies flicker, their glow oh-so-bright.
Here, fun never ends, it's a silly affair,
Where crickets and sea breeze float joy in the air.

Currents of Constant Change

Waves tumble like laughter, a comical dance,
As jellyfish sway, lost in a trance.
Starfish throw parties on sunken hulls,
With tempers as lively as seaweed's curls.

The tides have their moods, it's true, it's a fact,
One minute they're calm, the next they attack.
Hermit crabs gossip in shells far too tight,
Claiming their turf with imaginary might.

Each tide's a surprise, a whimsical ride,
As seashells enlist in the ocean's wild tide.
They whisper their secrets, tales of delight,
Where waves play tag with the shimmering light.

In this realm of change, we float and we roam,
With a grin on our faces, the sea feels like home.
So let's ride the currents, no time to be strange,
In this marvelous water, we embrace the change.

Dreams Cast in Shells

On the shore where wishes and foam intertwine,
Shells gather secrets, each one a design.
With dreams that shimmer like pearls in the bay,
They giggle and wink in a whimsical way.

Fish play charades in a watery guise,
While crabs throw confetti as starfish high-five.
With laughter and waves crashing soft on the beach,
Every moment a treasure, within easy reach.

The tides bring forth stories, both big and quite small,
As pelicans dive for their whimsical haul.
A dolphin named Dave does a flip with a cheer,
While sandpipers scamper, shedding a tear.

So gather your dreams and cast them on shells,
As the ocean invites us to share all our spells.
With merriment floating, we're never too far,
In this joyful sea, we shine like a star.

Celestial Currents

Fish in tuxedos, they dance with glee,
Bubbles burst like laughter, oh what a spree!
Seahorses spinning, a waltz in the tide,
Crabby comedians, with shells filled with pride.

Mermaids munch on seaweed snacks,
Jellyfish float with their jelly-filled packs.
Starfish on stilts, they throw a big bash,
While octopuses juggle, oh what a splash!

Waves clap their hands, a foamy applause,
Dolphins wear shades, they follow the laws.
Along comes a whale, singing tunes quite absurd,
While all the sea creatures can't help but be stirred.

Under the moon, they groove on the sand,
A party of fish, quite a sight so grand!
When tides come to play, all join the fun,
In this wacky world, there's no need to run.

Coral Dreams

Corals dressed up in tuxedo hues,
With anemones swaying, sharing their views.
Clownfish giggle, in their bubble parade,
While sea cucumbers serenade in the shade.

Shrimp play charades, with pearls as their props,
A crab plays the piano, it never stops.
Oysters tell tales of oceans so wide,
As the shimmering dolphins take a joyful ride.

The seaweed sways like hair with a flair,
While sea turtles wear hats, oh what a rare pair!
A starfish with sunglasses plays hide and seek,
Underwater shenanigans, so unique!

With laughter and bubbles, they dance in delight,
A carnival kingdom within the moonlight.
In depths of laughter, they splash and they beam,
Creating a ruckus, in their coral dream.

Beneath the Blue Veil

Under a veil where the dolphins do leap,
The sea whispers secrets, the crabs take a peep.
Jokes in the current, they ride with a grin,
Surprising a flounder, let the fun begin!

A turtle in flip-flops, slow but so cool,
Fish wearing capes, breaking every old rule.
The seaweed shakes its green hair in laughter,
As octopuses plot their next silly chapter.

Grouper in boots dances 'round the reef,
While clownfish crack jokes, bringing fish disbelief.
A plankton parade with tiny little flair,
Sways to the rhythm, without any care.

Under blue lighting, the party won't stop,
Where everyone's welcome, in this ocean bop.
With giggles and splashes, they frolic and play,
Silly and carefree, in their watery way.

Symphony of the Sea

An orchestra swims, notes in the breeze,
With conch shells singing, the waves burst with ease.
Clams strum the tunes, with a percussive clap,
While fish donned in bow ties take a gentle nap.

A whale conducts with a grand sweeping tail,
As seahorses trot in a tiny parade trail.
Shrimp play the flutes, and squid bang the drums,
Every coral and creature joyfully hums.

Sea turtles waltz to a rhythm so light,
Tangled-up seaweed guides with delight.
Jellyfish twirl like ballerinas in flow,
Proving that fun under water can glow!

With laughter and music, the sea sets the stage,
As bubbles float upward, they dance and engage.
A symphony crafted in cerulean sea,
Where parody sparkles, and all swim so free.

Home Among the Waves

Seagulls critique my beach attire,
Sunburned nose, I can aspire,
Sandcastles bow to ocean's might,
As crabs take over, what a sight!

Flip-flops fly with a splashy cheer,
Why did I step in that cold beer?
Fish do the cha-cha, what a show,
Whales auditioning for a TV show!

Jellyfish float with such finesse,
While I wobble in my sunburned mess,
Mermaids giggle as I take a dip,
Make sure the waves don't steal my chip!

Home among the waves, a wild spree,
Even the barnacles laugh at me,
Coconut drinks, oh what a tease,
Life's just a beach, if you please!

Tidal Reflections

Waves whisper secrets to the shore,
But my flip-flops are lost in galore,
Mirrors of water, sparkling tricks,
I see my face, and choose to nix!

Splashing and laughing, crabs place bets,
Spotting towels, and dodging pets,
Threw a beach ball, hit Uncle Fred,
Oh look, he's now a sand-angel spread!

Dolphins surf in perfect delight,
While I trip over a seashell, oh what a fright,
Starfish wave like they own the place,
While I channel my inner grace!

Reflections flicker, laugh-filled waves,
Chasing the tide, no one misbehaves,
Mermaids and I, we share a joke,
Life's a splash, come join the poke!

Gifts from the Deep

The ocean's treasures, what a mess,
A treasure chest filled with old dress,
Mermaids' relics, glittery scales,
And a message in a bottle that fails!

Crabby gifts come with a pinch,
I giggle as I see them clinch,
A tuba from a shellfish band,
Trying to jam with a grainy sand!

Octopuses have their own spa,
Waving their arms, they're quite the star,
But I brought snacks for this fine feast,
Prideful fish say, "No thanks, at least!"

Wrapped in seaweed, a gift for me,
"Take this clam," said a fish with glee,
Tasting the treasures, I burst out laughing,
Oceans provide, but what's worth grabbing?

A Sea of Stars

Starlit beaches with a twist of fate,
Finding starfish, collecting their plate,
I asked, "Why so shy?" They just winked,
Playing hide-and-seek with the moon, they linked!

The lighthouse twinkles with a grin,
As crabs dance off to a jazzy spin,
Fishermen's nets catch whispers of dreams,
And fish wear shades, or so it seems!

Sailing on laughter, waves in a whirl,
Finding beach balls gives my head a twirl,
Stars in the sky wink back at me,
While jellybeans float, wild and free!

A sea of stars, no need for light,
Every flip-flop tiptoes with delight,
Crashing waves sing a song so sweet,
Under the shimmering sky, life's a treat!

Embrace of the Deep

On a fish-shaped boat we ride,
With a seagull as our guide.
It squawks jokes about the tide,
As we drift and laugh, wide-eyed.

Bubbles rise in silly shows,
Tickling toes that splash like pros.
A crab does the cha-cha, who knows?
Is this a dance? Oh, how it glows!

The octopus juggles shells with glee,
While clams sing loudly just for me.
"Who's got the moves?" I yell in spree,
The seaweed sways in harmony.

With jellyfish gliding all about,
Their glow-in-the-dark disco routes.
We join the party, scream, and shout,
As waves applaud our silly clouts.

Dancing with Dolphins

Under the sun, we spin and sway,
With dolphins showing us their play.
They flip and dive, oh what a day,
I take a plunge—then drift away!

Splashing water, giggles abound,
A dolphin steals my hat, so proud.
"I'll get it back!" I shout aloud,
They bubble-laugh, it's quite the crowd!

With silly prances, they tease my feet,
While I attempt a two-step beat.
A belly flop—the ultimate feat,
The dolphins cheer, "That's hard to beat!"

As the sun sinks on this wild spree,
I thank the fins for dancing free.
And as they whistle back to sea,
I find my hat—just wait for me!

Shores of Serenity

On tranquil sands, we build a throne,
A castle made of seaweed grown.
The tide comes in, our laughter's shown,
As waves declare, "This place is known!"

A crab in a tux comes to inspect,
With sandy shoes, quite the effect.
"Who loves the dress code?" I suspect,
The seagulls caw, they stand correct.

With sunburned noses, sunscreen galore,
We try to balance on a boogie board.
I stumble, flop, but can't ignore
The laughter ringing from the shore.

The sunsets drape a golden glow,
As pirates in flip-flops steal the show.
With sandy snacks in tow, we know,
These shores bring joy, just like a pro!

Echoes of the Abyss

In the deep blue, where shadows creep,
I found a treasure chest—with a sheep!
"Why are you here? What's the leap?"
   It baas, then dives into a heap.

With fishy friends, I start a plot,
To train a dolphin to be a bot.
"Imagine the laughs! It's worth a shot!"
Together we swirl, laughter's caught.

Turtles wear hats, quite the style,
Waving hello with a toothy smile.
"Catch me if you can!" They swim a mile,
I splash behind, this is worthwhile!

Echoes bubble through coral scenes,
Where squid perform in sequined jeans.
I laugh, I dance, I burst the seams,
In this goofy world of fishy dreams.

Through the Eyes of a Sea Turtle

With a shell so grand, I glide with glee,
Swimming past fish, they wave at me.
Crabs try to dance, but trip on sand,
I chuckle and drift, my fate is planned.

Jellyfish float in a wobbly show,
They'd win the crown for the silliest flow.
I nibble on sea grass, oh what a feast,
While octopuses play tag, to say the least.

Currents tug me in a funny twist,
Racing with dolphins, they can't resist.
My slow-motion saga, a turtle's delight,
I wave at the waves – it's a silly sight!

The ocean's a circus, with laughter so loud,
I'm the star performer, in my shell, so proud.
Turtle tumbles and seaweed ballet,
Life's just a joke, come swim and play!

Dreams in the Drifting Dunes

The sand's a blanket, soft and warm,
I dream of mermaids, without a qualm.
Seagulls gossip, flying high above,
Plotting their antics, oh what a love!

Starfish come dancing, wearing bright jives,
They twinkle their arms; oh, what quirky lives!
The tide tries to tickle, oh what a tease,
But I laugh it off, like a playful breeze.

Shells with secrets whispering tales,
Of snails racing crabs with shimmering sails.
A clam sings a song, a crusty old tune,
Joining the laughter beneath the moon.

Sandcastles giggle, as waves pull them back,
"Hold tight, little tower!" they rustle and crack.
I drift in the dusk, with sand in my toes,
Wishing for laughter wherever it goes!

The Fisherman's Fantasy

Old Joe casts his line with a wink,
"Catch of the day? I can't even think!"
A fish jumps high, gives him a start,
Then splashes down, breaking his heart!

Fish gather round for an oceanic chat,
"Should we nibble the bait or just play pat?"
The hooks are a hoot, they wriggle in glee,
"Let's prank old Joe, swim wild and free!"

He wrestles his rod, oh what a scene,
With seaweed and laughter, it's all quite routine.
His hats get snagged on a passing whale,
"Oh no! Not my best hat, I'm doomed to fail."

But every cast lands a joke, it seems,
With pint-sized pufferfish filling his dreams.
With every splash, he grins with delight,
For fishing is fun, and what a sight!

Mermaids at Twilight

Under the stars, they twinkle and splash,
Mermaids in chorus, making a crash.
With glittering tails and giggles so bright,
They dance through the water, a magical sight.

A lobster plays piano, quite out of tune,
While gulls steal the show, they lip-sync to the moon.
Their seaweed wigs waving, oh what a flair,
The ocean's a cabaret, laughter in air!

They dive into bubbles, blow kisses around,
While seashells applaud with a clapping sound.
Each flip and each splash is a riot of fun,
With a wink from the waves, the show's just begun.

As twilight embraces, the laughter won't cease,
For in this wet wonderland, joy finds its peace.
Mermaids and sea creatures, all come to play,
In the shimmery waters, where dreams float away!

Where the Fish Whisper

In the deep where fish convene,
They gossip like a sneaky scene.
A grouper's joke, a clownfish grin,
All while the sea turtles spin.

A puffer fish told a tale,
Of a sailor who lost his sail.
Laughing waves with salty sprays,
Made all the octopuses sway.

A crab with style struts the floor,
Wearing shells as much as he wore.
He danced like no one was about,
Making all sea urchins shout.

So come on down, join the fun,
In the ocean, we all run!
For every fish has a quirk,
In this place where giggles lurk.

Jellyfish Lullabies

Gliding through with tentacle grace,
Jellyfish sing in a slow embrace.
They float and sway, soft as a sigh,
With zany tunes that mystify.

One jelly sings, "I lost my hat!"
Another laughs, "It's a floating mat!"
With laughter bubbling like the sea foam,
They create a watery home.

In this oceanic serenade,
The seahorses dance, undismayed.
Bubbles rise with every slap,
As fishes giggle in a nap.

With jelly lullabies so sweet,
The underwater crowd won't take a seat.
For when the tide decides to play,
You better join in this fishy ballet!

Lifeblood of the Ocean

In a coral reef, the party starts,
With rainbow fish and silly hearts.
The seaweed sways, like it's in trance,
While shrimp serve snacks—well, they dance!

A whale hums tunes of olden days,
While dolphins splash in playful ways.
They giggle as they dive and twist,
Making waves in a watery mist.

Anemones tickle the fins that pass,
While crabs throw shells like bits of glass.
What's a party without some fun?
Even the sea cucumbers run!

So raise a fin! Let's celebrate,
In this ocean, we can create.
With laughter as our lifeblood flow,
Together, we'll bask in the glow.

A Shell's Silent Story

Upon the shore, a shell does smile,
It's seen the ocean's grandest style.
With memories nestled deep inside,
Of waves that tickle and take on rides.

It whispers tales of passing boats,
And silly fish dressed up in coats.
The sea winds blow—what a delight,
As seagulls swoop in their silly flight.

Each crack and line a secret told,
Of underwater treasures bold.
A starfish snail with dreams to roam,
Turns sunset into a cozy home.

So find a shell upon the sand,
And listen close—take its hand.
In every crevice, laughter hides,
In the stories that the ocean provides.

Tidal Kaleidoscope

Waves are like jelly, all wobbly and bright,
A fish wearing glasses, oh what a sight!
Seagulls play poker on the drifting sands,
While crabs do the cha-cha, clapping their hands.

Starfish are quiet, but they know how to smile,
They've seen the whole sea, traveled many a mile.
With dolphins who giggle, flipping around,
The ocean's a playground where joy can be found.

Shells sing out tunes in a soft, breezy hum,
As turtles wear hats, calling each other 'chum.'
The seaweed does a limbo, swaying in glee,
And octopuses dance, oh so carefree!

Bubbles like giggles, float up to the sky,
While crabs make a fuss, "Who can dance high?"
The tide rolls with laughter, a comical scene,
In this underwater circus, oh, how they preen!

Mariner's Reverie

Once upon a sailboat, a cat took the wheel,
With waves that were laughing, oh what a deal!
Fish in tuxedos swim past with a grin,
While barnacles giggle, "Come join in the din!"

The compass is spinning, never quite still,
While sea monsters argue, "Who's next for the grill?"
A parrot sings opera, so loud and so free,
And mermaids join in with a cup of sweet tea.

Navigating laughter, they sailed on a whim,
With a map made of pudding, can you believe him?
The stars twinkled brightly, playing hide and seek,
As sailors sang ballads that were truly unique.

In the harbor, the boats wear their funny hats,
While crabs hold a meeting with some old sea rats.
The ocean's a party, with joy on the rise,
Where even the tides are full of surprise!

Enchanted Reefs

Beneath the blue waves, where mermaids reside,
Is a clamor of colors, and laughter won't hide.
Coral grows pipes, plays jazz through the night,
As fish spin a tale, full of giggles and light.

The jellyfish float like balloons in a spree,
While sea cucumbers contemplate what it could be.
The shrimp have a party, on a disco ball floor,
While clams do a shuffle, shelling out lore.

Starry-eyed fishes, with dreams big and bold,
Swim past a sea turtle, wearing marigold.
The currents are swaying with ticklish delight,
As lobsters perform a grand tap dance so tight.

In the heart of these reefs, where chaos reigns fun,
The sea critters giggle, when day turns to sun.
A cacophony sparkles, a riotous scene,
An aquarium of laughter, forever serene!

Journey to the Aquatic Isle

Let's pack up our laughter, set sails to the sound,
Where fish toss confetti, and joy knows no bound.
With seashells for trumpets, they'll welcome us here,
On the shores of a dream, where laughter's sincere.

The captain's a walrus, with wisdom galore,
He tells funny stories, we beg him for more.
As we float past the bubbles, all shiny and bright,
The dolphins start juggling, what a hilarious sight!

Crabs share their secrets in whimsical tone,
While sea urchins gossip, and no one's alone.
With wind in our sails, let's ride the big waves,
To the isle where we'll dance, just like freedom craves.

We'll feast on sea cucumbers, grilled with a wink,
As mermaids serve cocktails that bubble and clink.
Under palm trees that chuckle, our hearts full of glee,
This journey and laughter belong to the sea!

Lullabies from the Deep

Bubbles sing a tune, quite absurd,
Fish slap their tails, spreading the word.
Crabs dance in shoes that are far too tight,
While jellyfish glow like stars in the night.

Octopus plays games, he's quite a cheat,
He tickles the clams, oh, what a feat!
Seahorses gossip, tails intertwined,
As the ocean giggles, what a wild find!

Seaweed sways, a shimmy and shake,
Turtles throw parties for goodness' sake.
Starfish tell jokes, all laugh till they squeal,
In the depths below, it's quite the reel!

Anemones wiggle, feeling so spry,
With shells for hats, they dance and they fly.
Through waters deep, here joy never ends,
With laughter and bubbles, and all of its friends.

The Call of Wondrous Waters

Oh mighty waves, they wave back at you,
With splashes of laughter, a watery crew.
Mermaids whisper secrets, with giggles so bright,
Barrels of giggles bubble through the night.

Dolphins crack jokes, flipping with glee,
While barnacles snicker, "Oh, let's have tea!"
Sea cucumbers roll, say, 'We're in the mood,'
For a party so wild, it's totally rude!

The sea otters juggle, they aren't very good,
But everyone laughs, that's understood.
With shells as their drums, they beat out a tune,
Join in the fun, beneath the full moon.

Sardines and mackerel, each take a chance,
To show off a kick or a dazzling dance.
The rawness of joy is a wave we adore,
In waters so bright, who could ask for more?

Seraphs in Seafoam

From depths of blue, a giggle ascends,
A chorus of whales that just want to be friends.
With foam on their heads and a song in the air,
They shimmy through currents, without a care!

Crabby comedians tell puns with a snap,
While sea urchins roll, taking a nap.
Pufferfish puff up, looking quite sly,
As mermaids burst out with a bubbly reply!

The corals join in, with colors so bright,
Painting the scene, a whimsical sight.
They twirl in the currents, a fiesta of hue,
Underwater laughter spills forth like a brew.

So if ever you wander where giggles abound,
Dive into waters where joy can be found.
In seafoam they prance, these seraphs of fun,
In a world filled with laughter, we all can run!

Endless Horizons of Bliss

Upon endless waves where the sillies reside,
The fishes wear glasses, with laughs, they glide.
Seagulls in tutus prance through the sky,
While starfish throw confetti, oh my, oh my!

The plankton are dancing, they wiggle and sway,
As shrimp crack some jokes to brighten the day.
With playful camaraderie, friends swim along,
In the tides of good humor, they all sing a song.

Squids play charades, oh what a sight,
While turtles take selfies, feeling just right.
The sunbeams sparkle, a whimsical kiss,
As the ocean embraces this moment of bliss.

Here in the waves, let your spirit soar high,
With laughter on lips, as the dolphins fly by.
In this world of joy, let worries release,
In the heart of the sea, you'll find perfect peace.

A Realm of Boundless Blue

Fish in tuxedos dance and twirl,
Seashells gossip as they whirl.
Octopuses juggle with some flair,
While seagulls steal snacks from the air.

Crabs wearing hats with stripes so wide,
Race each other full of pride.
Starfish sunbathe on the sand,
Doing yoga—what a sight so grand!

Jellyfish float, all in a trance,
With wriggly tentacles, they prance.
Dolphins laugh in playful glee,
Thinking, 'How silly can fish be?'

A whale's loud burp shakes the sea floor,
What a ruckus; oh, what a roar!
In this realm, every wave's a laugh,
Where silliness reigns—come join the craft!

Muses of the Marine Mystique

Mermaids giggle with scales that shine,
Sharing secrets in waves, sipping brine.
Turtles in shades go for a ride,
Excitedly folding flippers wide.

Anemones act like bouncers in style,
Defending their patch with a wiggly smile.
Fish throw a party—uninvited, of course,
But everyone swims in without remorse!

Eels in tuxes serve jellybean bites,
Hiding 'neath coral on super slick nights.
A crab pulls a prank, hides in some kelp,
Shock and laughter make everyone yelp!

So come take a dip in this wild delight,
Where mischief and giggles make everything bright.
With mermaids and fish who can't help but grin,
This aquatic spectacle is where fun begins!

Where Sea and Sky Embrace

Clouds like cotton candy float on high,
Seagulls swoop down, aiming for pie.
Waves do the cha-cha, splashing with glee,
Dancing together in jubilee!

A clam with a grin plays a bold game,
Hiding a pearl, but no one can blame.
With waves as the music, and sand as the floor,
Sea creatures gather, waiting for more.

Sandy toes and foolhardy flips,
Beaches echo with laughter and quips.
Fish wear sunglasses, lounging with pride,
While the sea breeze whispers—enjoy the ride!

So sail into skies painted bright,
Where every wave brings pure delight.
Here, beneath the sun's warm embrace,
Laughter and joy fill every space!

The Enchanted Reef Awakens

Coral castles with magical flair,
Where fish swirl beneath in their dazzling wear.
Blowfish puffed like balloons in the air,
Giggle as bubbles float without a care.

Seahorses prance in a royal parade,
Twisting and turning in their grand charade.
Each vertex of coral whispers a tune,
While crabs compose songs beneath a bright moon.

In wrecks where treasure is lost long ago,
Squid hold auditions, putting on a show.
Laughter erupts from each nook and cranny,
While starfish debate who's the mightiest manny!

With each wave that crashes with zest,
Life in this reef is simply the best.
Bring your humor, dive deep and explore,
In this wondrous sea, you'll always want more!

www.ingramcontent.com/pod-product-compliance
Lightning Source LLC
Chambersburg PA
CBHW072220070526
44585CB00015B/1427